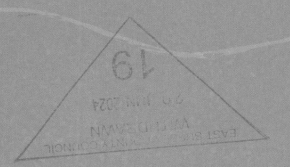

19

2 0 JUN 2024
WITHDRAWN
EAST SUSSEX COUNTY COUNCIL

D1333217

04641254

PUBERTY in NUMBERS

LIZ FLAVELL

W
FRANKLIN WATTS
LONDON • SYDNEY

Franklin Watts
First published in Great Britain in 2019 by The Watts Publishing Group
Copyright © The Watts Publishing Group, 2019

All rights reserved.

HB ISBN: 978 1 4451 6391 8
PB ISBN: 978 1 4451 6392 5

Printed in Dubai

MIX
Paper from
responsible sources
FSC® C104740

Series Editor: Amy Pimperton
Design and Illustration: Collaborate

Franklin Watts
An imprint of
Hachette Children's Group
Part of The Watts Publishing Group
Carmelite House
50 Victoria Embankment
London EC4Y 0DZ
An Hachette UK Company

www.hachette.co.uk
www.franklinwatts.co.uk

The facts and figures in this book were correct at the time of printing.

The websites (URLS) included in this book were valid at the time of going to press. However, it is possible
that the contents or addresses may have changed since the publication of this book. No responsibility for
any such changes can be accepted by either the author or the Publisher.

CONTENTS

For the purposes of this book, we have used the following terms to distinguish between male and female in relation to their sexual reproductive systems and organs, not their gender identity.

 FEMALE (GIRL)
a person born with (usually)
a vagina and ovaries,
and produces eggs

MALE (BOY)
a person born with (usually)
a penis and testes,
and produces sperm

For gender see pages 32–33.

NO PROBLEM, IT'S JUST PUBERTY

80 AWKWARD MOMENTS EVERY DAY!

Puberty and embarrassment go hand in hand. Changes happening to your body can be worrying or confusing and comments about your appearance or questions about your personal life can make you feel uncomfortable. You might experience puberty-related awkwardness up to **80 times a day**, but don't worry, you *will* be able to handle it!

NUMBER ONE ENEMIES

Embarrassment and feeling awkward are your **number one enemies** when it comes to puberty, but YOU DO NOT NEED TO BE EMBARRASSED! At some stage, everyone goes through it.

This book will show you that learning about our bodies and emotions during puberty is fascinating. All bodies are brilliant and growing up is a great adventure. All around the world, millions of young people are going through the same thing. Puberty really is nothing to fear.

PICK A NUMBER

What would you do in this situation? You're with some friends – including that person you really, really like – and someone turns to you and says, 'Have you snogged anyone yet?'.

1. make a swift exit before anyone sees you blush

2. crack a rubbish joke

3. start rapping – badly

4. ignore all questions and talk about something else instead

5. stuff this book up your jumper and read it secretly to get some advice

6. smile and say, 'Absolutely none of your business!'.

If you answered **5** or **6** then well done. If you ticked anything else, help is on its way …

WHAT IS PUBERTY?

So what is all the fuss about? Simply put: puberty is when a child's body changes into an adult's. If that sounds scary then remember, it's a gradual thing. Usually, your body kicks into action anywhere between the **ages of 8 and 15** but it can take a few years for the whole puberty thing to happen. At the end of it all, you will probably have a body that is ready to reproduce – make babies – if you want to.

UP-CLOSE AND PERSONAL

Your body will go through lots of changes during puberty. Things may kick off with hair on your face (boys, and girls too sometimes!), under your arms *and* down there! Boys' penises gradually grow bigger. Girls' breasts begin to develop. Everyone gets mad mood swings. So much is going on inside and out it's not surprising we feel a bit overwhelmed, but it's all part of the journey that is puberty.

PERIODS   SCROTUM   NIPPLES

PENIS   LABIA   VAGINA

EJACULATION

EGGS   **Get to grips with these puberty-related words to help you overcome any embarrassment.**   OVARIES

CLITORIS   ORGASM

SEX   SPERM   BREASTS   FORESKIN

TESTICLES   PUBIC HAIR   CHEST

VULVA   HORMONES

AMAZING BODY NUMBERS

Babies can't happen without the menstrual cycle and sex cells. Male sex cells are called sperm and female sex cells are called eggs.

The average female is born with about **2 MILLION EGGS**.

There are **200–500 MILLION SPERM** in each **EJACULATION**.

The average male produces **525 BILLION SPERM** in a lifetime.

The average **MENSTRUAL CYCLE** lasts **21–35 DAYS**.

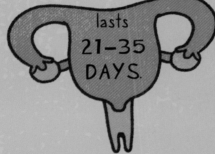

Eggs are the **LARGEST CELLS** in the human body.

WEIRD AND WONDERFUL NATURE

If you think your body is weird and embarrassing, then these facts and figures from the animal kingdom will make you think again!

- blue whales have the biggest penises – over **2 m long**
- the shrewish short-tailed opossum from South America has the most nipples of any animal – up to **27**
- female Napoleon wrasse (fish), **can change sex** to become male
- the longest pregnancy belongs to the Indian elephant at **22 months**.

COUNTDOWN TO PUBERTY
5-4-3-2-1 ... LIFT OFF!

During the countdown to puberty a whoosh of hormones hits your body. It's a time of amazing changes. These hormones are powerful and they are entirely natural. Your body is designed to receive them, but what are these hormones up to?

30 POWERFUL HORMONES

Hormones are substances made by glands in the body. There are believed to be around **30 different kinds of hormone** that affect our bodies during puberty. Each one does a different job.

Three hormones trigger puberty. Don't panic, it doesn't result in one big explosion causing puberty to happen overnight. The hormones enter your bloodstream slowly and work while you're asleep! As puberty progresses, they start working **24/7** and that's when all the major changes begin.

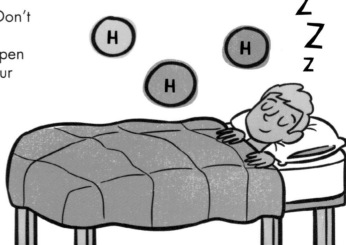

WHAT DO PUBERTY HORMONES DO?

They enter the glands in either the testicles or the ovaries and sort of wake them up! This stimulates the production of two more hormones – **testosterone** and **oestrogen** – in both boys and girls. Boys tend to produce more testosterone and girls more oestrogen. These two hormones are key to many of the bodily changes during puberty.

WHEN WILL IT HAPPEN?

Everyone would like to know precisely when they will enter puberty, but there is no exact age. Anywhere between **8 to 17** is normal. Try not to worry, puberty will begin when it's ready.

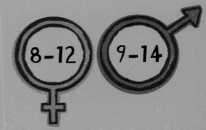

8–12   9–14

HOW LONG WILL IT TAKE?

Puberty takes a few years, so you will have plenty of time to adjust to the changes as they happen.

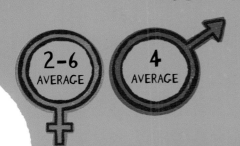

2–6 AVERAGE   4 AVERAGE

LADIES FIRST

WHAT HAPPENS WHEN?

Puberty usually starts earlier for girls. Once the hormones get to work, things start happening. The order in which changes arrive is different for everyone, but whatever happens, rest assured you are normal. You might notice hair growing somewhere other than your head or your breasts developing — and that's just on the outside. There are other things going on inside.

THE 1-2-3 OF BODY CHANGES

1. THINGS YOU CAN SEE

1. growth spurts

2. breast buds develop into breasts

3. armpit hair grows

4. pubic hair grows

5. hips grow wider

6. legs get hairier

7. feet and hands get bigger

8. skin gets greasier and you may have spots or acne.

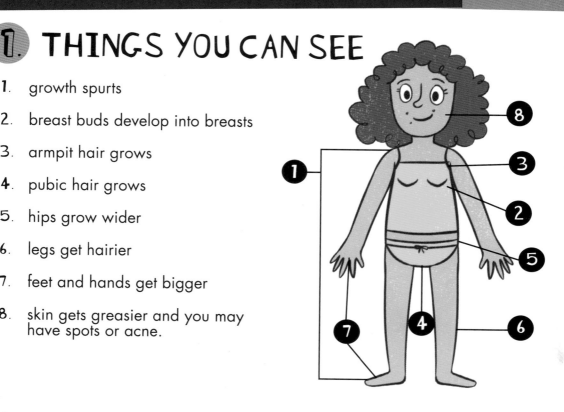

2. ON THE INSIDE

Inside the average female there is a network of body parts and tubes known as the female sex organs. This is called the sexual reproduction system and it is designed to make babies. Sexual reproduction is when a male sex cell (sperm) and a female sex cell (egg) join together inside the female reproductive system in order to create a new life. During puberty these organs will grow larger as you grow, but you won't feel this.

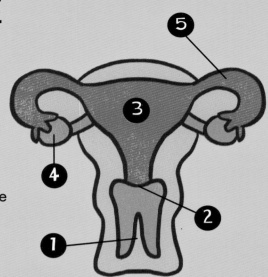

1. **vagina**: this tube connects the internal sex organs to the external sex organs.
2. **cervix**: this is the entrance to the uterus.
3. **uterus** (womb): a foetus (baby) develops here during pregnancy.

4. **ovaries**: this is where unfertilised eggs are stored.
5. **fallopian tubes**: an egg travels from an ovary through **one of the 2 fallopian tubes** to the uterus.

REPRODUCTION SYSTEM STATS

- the uterus is around **7.5 cm long** and **5 cm wide**
- fallopian tubes measure about **10 cm long**
- the vagina is a stretchy tube that varies in size – anything from **7.6–17.7 cm**.

3. ALL IN YOUR HEAD

Some changes you can't see are those that you will feel. Puberty can make you more aware of how your body feels. Your emotions can be affected by all the physical and hormonal changes.

ALL SHAPES AND SIZES

Female genitals are amazing, both inside and out. Whether you call it a front bottom, a twinkle or whatever word you use, it's not just for weeing. There are many parts that are all really interesting.

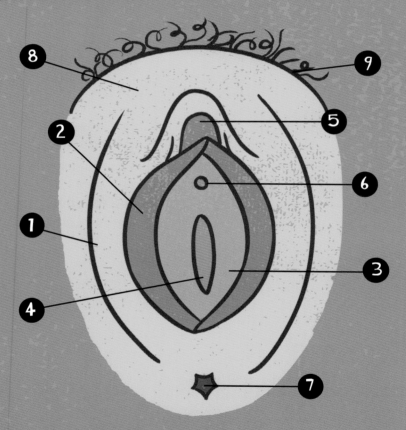

9 VULVA PARTS

The bits you can see are the external sex organs (also called the vulva or genitals). They are the gateway to all the important baby-making stuff. Genitals come in all shapes and sizes and no one should feel ashamed of how they look. Everyone is different.

TWICE AS NICE

The clitoris has around **7,000–8,000 nerve endings.** This is twice as many as the average penis, which has around **4,000 nerve endings.**

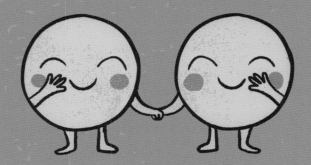

SUPER-STRETCHY

The vagina is on the inside and this organ has amazing superpowers. It can stretch and expand to over **200 times its normal size!** This is important because this tube is where babies leave the womb.

1. **outer labia**: these folds (lips) of skin protect the vulva.

2. **inner labia**: these sensitive folds of skin also protect the vulva.

3. **vagina opening**

4. **vagina entrance**

5. **clitoris**: this is a sensitive bundle of nerve endings, which when touched can feel nice.

6. **urethral opening**: this is the small hole where wee comes out of.

7. **anus**: this is the hole where poo comes out of.

8. **mons pubis**: this mound of fatty tissue covers and protects the pubic area (it is also called the pubic mound).

9. **pubic hair**.

ALL ABOUT BREASTS

Usually, one of the first visible body changes is when the breasts begin to grow. This can happen earlier than **age 9** or later than **age 11** – it's unique to you! The age it starts happening doesn't affect the size they will end up. Amazingly, breast development starts right back at birth.

5 STAGES OF BREAST DEVELOPMENT

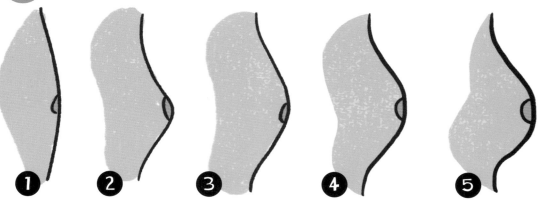

1 **2** **3** **4** **5**

This diagram shows an average development of breast size.
Yours may be smaller or larger than these.

5 THINGS TO GET OFF YOUR CHEST

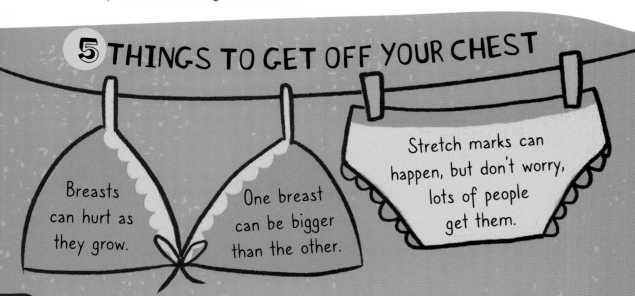

Breasts can hurt as they grow.

One breast can be bigger than the other.

Stretch marks can happen, but don't worry, lots of people get them.

STAGE 1: Birth to prepuberty

The tip of the nipple is raised and the chest area is flat.

STAGE 2: Prepuberty

Girls develop breast buds at around **9 to 10 years old**. These hard little lumps under the nipple can feel tender. The area around the nipple (areola) may get bigger and darker, too.

STAGE 3: Early puberty

As more breast tissue develops, the breasts increase in size.

STAGE 4: Late puberty

The nipple and the areola grow and may stick out from the breast.

STAGE 5: Adulthood

Breasts are fully developed by about the **age of 20**. They will vary throughout life, depending on childbirth, weight changes, age and hormones.

626 ml

WHAT ARE BREASTS FOR?

Breasts and nipples are designed to make milk to feed babies. The proper word for this is lactation. Breast milk is the perfect food for babies because it contains over **200 vitamins**. A baby weighing **4 kg** needs around **626 ml of breast milk per day**, which is about the same as a very large glass of milk.

Nipples can be round, oval, small or large – all are normal.

You may have hair around your nipples – this is normal, too!

BRAVING BRA BUYING

32B OR NOT 32B, THAT IS THE QUESTION!

Buying a bra for the first time IS a big deal. Some girls leap around with joy at the thought. Others find underwear departments seriously scary places. There are sports bras, underwired ones, seamless ones, plain ones and patterned ones. Shopping for bras can feel ultra-embarrassing. So, how do you find the bra that is right for you?

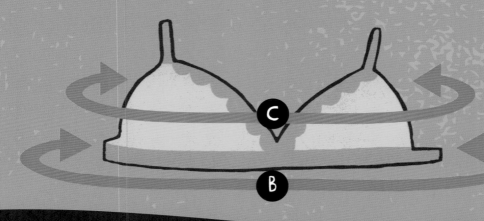

EASY AS AA-B-C-DD

A. Everybody should get measured properly before they buy a bra. Many shops have experts who are trained to do this.

B. First, a measurement is taken around the ribcage to find your chest size. Bras are still measured mostly in inches.

C. Next, a measurement is taken around the breast. This shows the cup size which can vary anywhere from AA (smallest) to LL (largest).

D. Try on lots of bras to find one that fits properly. Comfort is a must and it should provide proper support while the breasts grow.

A QUICK WORD ABOUT HAIR
DOWN THERE!

Let's get this straight (or curly), pubic hair happens. It develops over time into a triangle-shaped patch that covers the pubis mons, the scrotum or vulva and sometimes the tops of your thighs.

EVERYWHERE

During puberty hair crops up on your legs, face and other parts of your body, and under your arms. It's natural, so there's no need to rush off to the bathroom to shave it off. Talk to an adult, get advice and think twice. And remember, you have hair down there and everywhere for a reason.

⑤ FURRY FACTS

1. Pubic hair protects. Think of it as a fluffy blanket that protects the delicate skin from friction. It also helps prevent bacteria from entering the vagina.

2. It helps to absorb sweat.

3. It has always been there – it was just short and fine when you were very young.

4. It doesn't always match the colour of the hair on the head.

5. Pubic hair grows by around **0.5 mm** every day.

TIME OF THE MONTH

Worrying about when your first period will start is normal. On average it happens around **12 to 18 months** after the breasts start growing — there is no precise science here. Don't worry — unless you tell everyone, nobody will know you are on your period! Another concern is what to use when there are so many pads, tampons and menstrual cups to choose from. Talk to a trusted adult about this or anything about periods that worries you.

CAUSE TO CELEBRATE

Having your period is also called menstruation. Your **first period** is technically known as the menarch. That word sounds like 'monarch', so be like a queen and celebrate this special time — many cultures around the world do!

Menstuation usually happens **once a month**. It's a good idea to note down the day it starts in a calendar or diary.

THE MENSTRUAL CYCLE

The average cycle lasts **28 days**, but remember it varies from person to person.

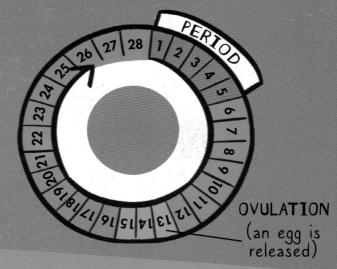

PERIOD

OVULATION
(an egg is released)

ANYTHING GOES

- average age of periods starting is **13 years**
- blood loss: **30–40 ml**, which is about **4–8 teaspoons**
- periods can last anything from **2–7 days**. The average is **5 days**.
- an average-sized pad or tampon can absorb **5 ml** of blood
- a menstrual cycle lasts between **23–35 days**.

5 ANNOYING THINGS ABOUT PERIODS

Girls often feel and can look different just before the start of each period. This is called premenstrual syndrome (PMS). You might experience:

1. mood swings
2. acne
3. aches and pains (cramps) down there
4. bloated stomach
5. headache.

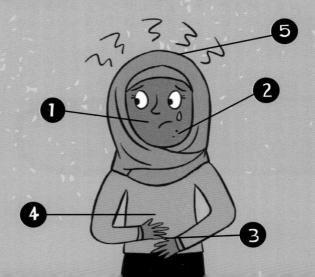

BOYS AND THEIR BITS

When a boy hits puberty, one of the first signs, along with pubic hair (see page 17), is that the testicles and penis grow bigger. These changes happen around **ages 12 to 16**. Penises come in all shapes and sizes and all are perfectly normal. Penises tend to get hard and erect wherever and whenever they like, in a phenomenon called spontaneous erections. Don't worry, over time this should happen less often.

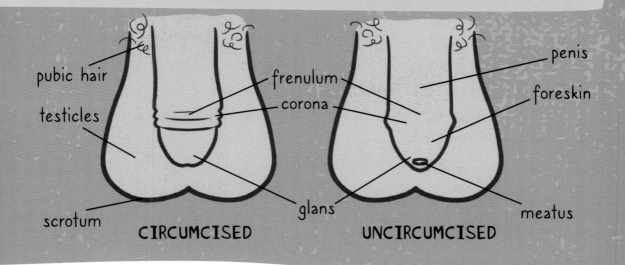

pubic hair

testicles

scrotum

frenulum

corona

glans

CIRCUMCISED

penis

foreskin

meatus

UNCIRCUMCISED

GENIUS PENIS FACTS

Most men have a fully developed penis size by **age 18 to 21**.

The average man can have **8–11 ERECTIONS** each day.

During an erection, about **100 ml of BLOOD** fills **3 CYLINDERS** of **ERECTILE TISSUE** inside the penis.

THE CIRCUMCISION DECISION

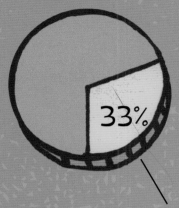

33%

Circumcision is the removal of the foreskin. It is a medical procedure, so it should be done in hospital by a surgeon. It is custom for many Jewish and Islamic boys to be circumcised. Sometimes it happens for medical reasons, such as having a foreskin that is too tight, which can make erections painful.

CIRCUMCISED MEN over the **AGE OF 15** (worldwide)

NOT A MEASURE OF MANHOOD

The average size of an erect penis is **13–18 cm** for an adult male, but size really doesn't matter. Remember, the size of a soft (flaccid) penis can be very different to an erect penis.

ERECT

FLACCID

Most spontaneous erections go away after a few minutes.

An erect penis can point upwards, outwards, downwards, to the side or it can be wonky.

Each ejaculation may have **1.25–5 ml** of **SEMEN**, which is about **0.25–1 TEASPOON**.

An average of **7 SPURTS** of semen and **10 CONTRACTIONS** afterwards occur for each ejaculation.

PEEING AND PLUMBING

The penis is used for peeing and for sexual reproduction — it's a very important bit of kit! But there are lots of other things going on inside a boy's body and it's not all about sex!

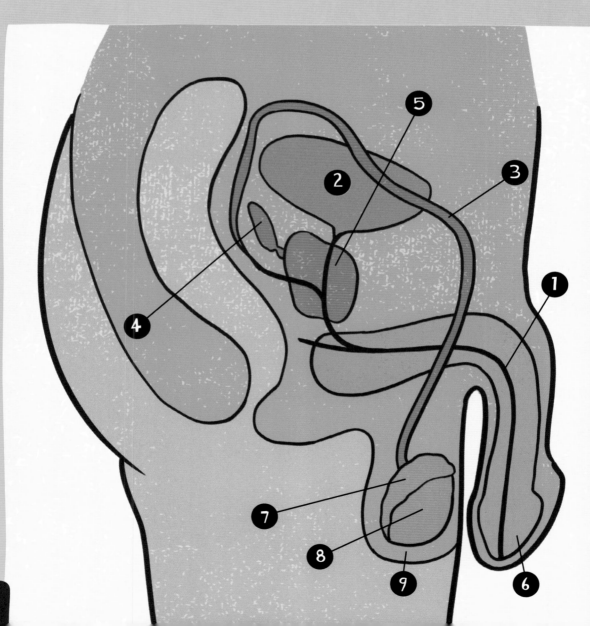

HOW COOL?

The body produces more sperm when the temperature of the testicles is around **3–5 °C** below body temperature, so it's important for reproduction that they stay cool. If the testicles get too hot, then the testicles hang lower to try and cool down. In cold temperatures, muscles pull the testicles up towards the body to get warmer.

1. **Urethra**: this tube carries wee and semen* to the end of the penis.

2. **Bladder**: part of the urinary system, this organ is where wee is stored.

3. **Vas deferens**: sperm travel along these tubes towards the seminal vesicles.

4. **Seminal vesicles**: around **70 per cent** of semen is produced here.

5. **Prostate gland**: around **30 per cent** of semen is produced here.

6. **Glans penis**: the end or 'head' of the penis. It has a small hole where wee and semen come out of.

7. **Epididymis**: sperm is stored here for around **4–5 weeks**.

8. **Testicles**: sperm and the hormone testosterone are produced in (usually) **2 testicles**.

9. **Scrotum**: this is the protective sack for the testicles.

* Semen is the fluid that contains sperm.

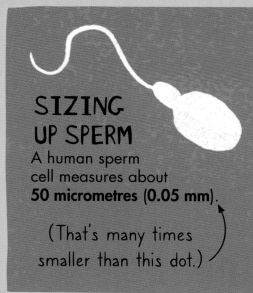

SIZING UP SPERM

A human sperm cell measures about **50 micrometres (0.05 mm)**.

(That's many times smaller than this dot.)

HOW FAST?

Speedy sperm exit the body during ejaculation at about **45 kph** on average.

GROWTH SPURTS AND BUM FLUFF

STRONGER, BIGGER, DEEPER

Most boys experience growth spurts where the chest and shoulders begin to develop and testosterone increases muscle size. Boys' voices start to break and become deeper as the larynx gets bigger. You may experience croaks and squeaks as your voice is breaking, but remember, this happens to everyone — there's no need to feel embarrassed.

GROWTH SPURTS

On average, between the **ages of 12 to 15**, boys will grow around **7–9 cm per year**. Growing taller quickly can make you feel clumsy at times, but it's simply your body getting used to its new longer limbs!

FROM BUM FLUFF TO BEARD

As boys grow so does their hair – everywhere! Hair will grow on your pubic area, arms and legs. Chest hair usually appears around **ages 13 to 18**, but some men may not have fully developed chest hair until they are **age 30** or even older, and some don't get any at all. Once testosterone kicks in, facial hair starts to grow.

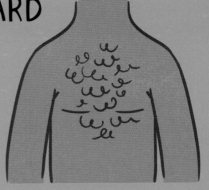

AGE 9–11: enjoy smooth baby-soft skin, although some boys may start puberty early and begin producing hair around now.

AGE 11–15: wispy hair (sometimes called 'bum fluff') appears above the top lip. You can shave it off if you want to.

AGE 16–18: Hair grows thicker and fuller. It may grow on the cheeks and under the lower lip. Some boys may shave every day.

AGE 18–21: Some boys can grow a full beard with sideburns. It may be time to experiment with length, style and thickness. However, not all men are able to grow beards.

3 FUZZY FACTS

1. The average beard grows by nearly **14 cm** every year.

2. Around the world, **55 per cent** of men have a beard or facial hair.

3. Shaving takes time! The average male who shaves will spend around **3,350 hours** shaving in a lifetime.

WET DREAMS

Boys and girls have a whirlwind of things going on during puberty. Bigger breasts and penises, hair sprouting everywhere, periods, moody meltdowns and lots of spots! For boys one of the most bewildering parts of growing up is 'night emissions' (wet dreams). But don't fret, if you wake up with a damp patch on your sheets, your body is doing exactly what it was designed to do. And, girls, you may get wet dreams too.

WHAT'S IN YOUR HEAD?

When you have a wet dream all kinds of things may go through your head. Sometimes you remember what you dreamed about and other times you have no idea. These dreams can make you feel excited or even guilty. Don't worry – these are only dreams and not necessarily what you like in the real world.

YOU ARE NOT ALONE!

- **80 per cent** of males have had a wet dream at one time in their life.

- **85 per cent** of females have had a 'wet dream' by the time they reach **21**.

THE WET DREAM Q & A

Q. WHAT IS A WET DREAM?

A. A wet dream is like an orgasm in your sleep.

Q. WHAT HAPPENS WHEN YOU HAVE A WET DREAM?

A. Males ejaculate semen. A female may have an orgasm and feel a bit wet, but probably won't stain the bed or their bed clothes.

Q. WHY DOES THIS HAPPEN?

A. Healthy sperm are needed to make healthy babies. Male bodies are designed to regularly get rid of old sperm to make way for new healthy sperm. Ejaculation is how males get rid of sperm.

TESTOSTERONE

THOUGHTS

During puberty, the surge of new hormones in your body make you think about sex more often. On average, teenage boys have an erection **4 times in one night**. They have many more during their waking hours too!

TOP TIP

Wear shorts to bed if you don't want to stain the sheets!

27

THE STINKY YEARS!

During puberty, around **3 million sweat glands** spring into action. Along with sweaty armpits, your genitals may smell, too. Being sweaty and stinky can feel unpleasant and embarrassing. Don't panic, with good hygiene you can combat it. Remember, sweating is a good thing; it's your body's way of cooling down, getting rid of unwanted chemicals and keeping you in tip-top condition.

A BIT WHIFFY!

There are **2 main kinds of sweat gland**. So if you're a bit whiffy, you know what to blame!

- **Eccrine glands:** found all over the body and especially on the head, palms and soles of the feet

- **Apocrine gland:** found mostly in very hairy places, such as the armpits and genitals. The sweat reacts with bacteria, which causes the smell.

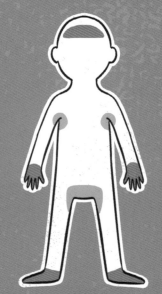

The eccrine glands can produce up to **10 LITRES** of **SWEAT** a day.

SWEAT CAUSED BY:

anxiety

temperature

activity

hormone changes

bacteria on the skin

diet

SWEAT COMBATED BY:

anti-perspirant

change of diet

regular washing

clean clothes

250,000 SWEAT GLANDS x bacteria x warm, dark trainer = **STINKY FEET!**

10–15 PER CENT of people have super-pongy feet.

KEEPING FRESH DOWN THERE

Sweat glands around the genitals secrete a substance called smegma. Often it has a thick, cheesy appearance and can smell. Washing every day is the best way to keep squeaky clean down there.

4 STEPS FOR BOYS

1. If you have one, pull the foreskin back gently – never force it.

2. Clean underneath with warm water and a mild, unperfumed soap. Do not scrub.

3. Rinse with clean water and gently pat dry.

4. If you have one, gently pull the foreskin back over the end of the penis.

4 STEPS FOR GIRLS

1. Vaginas are self-cleaning and don't need douches or vaginal wipes.

2. Wash around the vulva with mild unperfumed soap. Perfumes, gels and antiseptics can cause irritation or infections.

3. Wear cotton underwear. Polyester or nylon fabrics are less breathable than cotton.

4. Wipe from front to back to stop bacteria from your bottom entering the vagina.

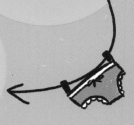

PIMPLES MADE SIMPLE

Acne, blackheads, spots and pimples are a fact of life during puberty. So, what are these dreaded things, what causes outbreaks of them and what can you do to make the whole situation better?

BLOCKS MEAN SPOTS

Sebum – an oil that is made in the sebaceous glands – is the root cause of spots. Hormones during puberty can cause sebum oil production to go crazy. These oils can block pores and trap bacteria, which in a matter of around **2 weeks** can become unsightly spots and annoying blackheads.

NO PIMPLE-POPPING

Keep your hands off your spots because you can spread bacteria and make them worse. You might also be left with scars on your skin. **You have been warned!**

ACNE ATTACKS

85%

of people between **12 and 24** get acne.

96%

of people with acne find it upsetting.

99%

of people with acne get acne on their face.

60%

of people with acne have acne on their body.

WHAT CAN YOU DO?

Spots are a normal sign of puberty, but you can help your body to fight the bacteria by doing a few simple things every day. If you have severe acne, you should see your doctor who may prescribe treatment.

MOISTURISE EXFOLIATE **WASH DAILY**

WASH YOUR HANDS OFTEN HEALTHY DIET TREATMENTS DON'T TOUCH THEM

 AVOID MAKE-UP GET MORE SLEEP

DIET MATTERS

Eating healthily won't stop spots, but it will help your body to fight against infection.

Eat **5–7 PORTIONS** of fruit and vegetables each day. Vitamins + minerals = cell renewal and glowing skin.

4–6 PORTIONS of carbohydrates and starches = top energy!

3 PORTIONS of calcium = healthy bones and teeth.

2–3 portions of protein = healthy tissues.

Drink **6–8 GLASSES** of water. Being hydrated helps your skin.

WHO AM I?
GENDER AND IDENTITY

Puberty brings with it many changes on the outside, but there's lots going on inside the head, too. Sometimes people find themselves confused and wondering about who they really are? What is their gender identity and how do they feel sexually?

IT'S ALL IN THE GENES

Your sex is determined by your chromosomes. In most cases these produce either male or female sexual reproductive systems. In some cases a person's sex is less distinct (see intersex on page 33). Gender identity relates to whether you decide you are a man or a woman (or both) and your identity may differ from your sex.

22 pairs of matched chromosomes +
Female: (2x) X chromosomes = XX
Male: (1x) X + (1x) y = Xy

+ HORMONES!!!!
= ANYTHING CAN HAPPEN!

112 GENDER IDENTITIES

The truth is you can be whoever you want to be. Just because you are born with certain sexual bits doesn't mean you feel like that person inside and it helps to understand that there are at least **112 gender identities***. Here are some of the more familiar ones …

CISGENDER

This is someone who is born a certain sex and identifies as that. If you were born with female sexual organs and consider yourself a woman then you are a cisgender woman.

TRANSGENDER

This is a person who is born a certain sex, but identifies otherwise. For example if you were born with male sexual organs, but identify as a woman, then you are a transgender woman.

AGENDER OR GENDER-NEUTRAL

This is somebody who doesn't feel that they belong to either gender.

QUESTIONING

This is a person who won't label themselves as either gender while they are exploring what they feel.

GENDER FLUID

This term covers a wide range of identities of people who feel like a mix of man and woman.

POLYGENDER

This is a person who identifies as several genders, either all at the same time or at different times.

OTHER

Non-binary is a term used to describe genders that don't fall into man or woman.

INTERSEX

Intersex is not a gender identity in itself. People who are intersex are born with genitalia that could be called male or female. Maybe they are born with genitals that appear female, but have male sexual organs inside. Intersex people generally identify with the gender that feels right for them.

* There are probably more, as definitions evolve all the time.

GAY, STRAIGHT, BI?

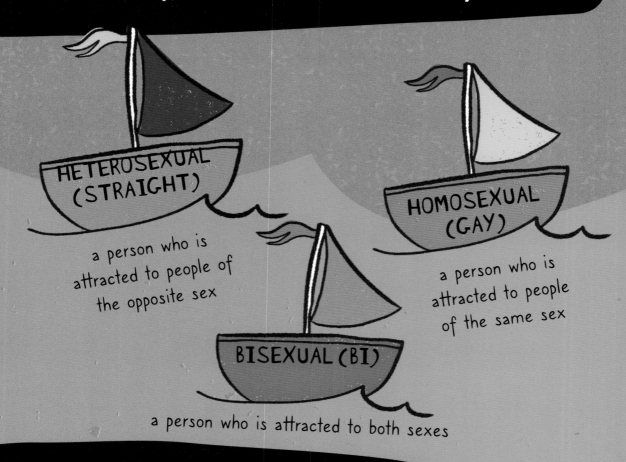

HETEROSEXUAL (STRAIGHT)

a person who is attracted to people of the opposite sex

HOMOSEXUAL (GAY)

a person who is attracted to people of the same sex

BISEXUAL (BI)

a person who is attracted to both sexes

SEXUAL IDENTITY

Puberty is an exciting time when young people experience more sexual feelings. You don't have much control over who you fancy. It takes time and experience to discover your sexual identity. Don't be in a rush to decide. You have your entire life to make up your mind, because how you feel at **12** might be completely different to how you feel at **18**, **30** or even **50+**. That's the brilliant thing about your sexuality — it isn't ever really **100 per cent** nailed down.

IT'S A VOYAGE OF DISCOVERY!

There are loads of different sexual identities – here are a few that are probably familiar.

a person who is attracted to people whatever their sex or gender

a person who isn't interested in having sex, but may have romantic relationships

a person who doesn't want a romantic connection but may still want sex

an umbrella term for anyone who isn't heterosexual

BULLYING

Nearly **50 per cent** of gay, bi and trans young people have been bullied because of their gender and/or sexuality. **92 per cent** of LGBTQI+ teens in a survey had experienced negativity about being gay, trans or questioning.

FIRST KISS

At some stage you're going to fancy somebody and you may want to ask them out. First dates, first kisses and first loves can feel brilliant, but take your time and make sure you are ready for what's happening to you. Don't feel pressured to do anything just because your friends are doing it.

FIRST CRUSH   FIRST DATE   **FIRST KISS?**   FIRST RELATIONSHIP   FIRST LOVE   FIRST BREAK-UP

you fret about asking *them* out

you keep looking at them

you get butterflies

you panic at the thought of them asking you out

8 SURE SIGNS YOU FANCY SOMEBODY

you can't stop thinking about them

you feel awkward and shy around them

you dream about them

you worry that your friends will out you!

PUCKER UP

EMBRACE

SNOG

FRENCH KISS

POUT

66 PER CENT of people tilt their head to the right when they kiss.

We use 34 FACIAL MUSCLES when we kiss.

The Guinness World Record for the longest kiss is 58 HOURS, 35 MINUTES AND 58 SECONDS.

LOCK LIPS

SMOOCH

CANOODLE

PECK

TO KISS OR NOT TO KISS?

- Out of **168 cultures** around the world only **46 per cent** kiss in a romantic way. Kissing seems to happen mostly in western countries.
- Chimpanzees and bonobos are amongst the few animals that kiss.

1,000,000 NERVE ENDINGS

The more than **1 million nerve endings** in our lips make them the most sensitive part of the body. Kissing feels good, but it also helps us to swap pheromones, which is nature's way of finding out if you are compatible with someone.

RESPECT YOURSELF (AND OTHERS)

Kissing is often one of the first steps towards a sexual relationship. It is really important to remember that kissing someone doesn't mean that you have to take things any further. It is always important to be respectful, kind, honest and safe. If you (or the person you are kissing) wants to stop, then you should stop. You have the right to say what happens to your body and you can withdraw your consent to be kissed or touched at any time.

MASTURBATION

Touching and rubbing your penis or clitoris is called masturbation and it isn't anything you should feel embarrassed about, but you should do it in private. During puberty, feelings of sexual pleasure from masturbation may grow and you may bring yourself to orgasm for the first time.

WHAT IS AN ORGASM?

Some would say that an orgasm (also called 'coming' or 'climaxing') is the peak of sexual satisfaction. The feeling has been described as a flood of sensations that radiate out from the genitals as the genital muscles contract and relax. Some say it's like an amazing explosion with lovely, tingly aftershocks. Everyone has a different experience – mostly good!

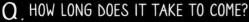

Q. HOW LONG DOES IT TAKE TO COME?

A. On average, it takes about **2–10 minutes** for a male to reach orgasm, but sometimes it's a matter of moments. It takes between **10–20 minutes** for a female to climax on average, but some climax within **30 seconds.**

On average, boys start masturbating at **12.5 YEARS.**

On average, girls start masturbating at **13.7 YEARS.**

WHY DO WE DO IT?

RELIEVE SEXUAL TENSION

SEXUAL PLEASURE

RELAXATION OR STRESS RELIEF

Z Z z

TO HELP YOU SLEEP

MASTURBATION – THE TRUTH!

Masturbation is a natural, positive and fun part of puberty, but it can be very awkward to discuss. Lots of people do it – around **78 per cent** of adults masturbate – but not many people want to talk about it. This can be down to cultural, religious or simply individual reasons.

5 GOOD THINGS ABOUT MASTURBATION

Masturbation is NOT bad for you. It won't stop you growing, send you crazy or make you go blind.

1. it's pleasurable

2. it can improve your health by boosting your immune system

3. you discover more about what you like sexually

4. it's ultra-safe as you can't get pregnant by masturbating

5. it's NORMAL and NATURAL.

LET'S TALK ABOUT SEX

All the changes happening during puberty are about making the body ready to have sex and make babies. Yet, having sex isn't just about reproduction. Sex can feel fun and exciting, so people do it because it feels pleasurable. It is important to be ready for it mentally as well as physically. However, sex should always be consensual; your choice and the choice of the person you do it with.

VIRGINITY

Somebody who has not had sexual intercourse is called a virgin. When a person has sexual intercourse for the first time, some people say they have 'lost their virginity'.

THE AGE OF CONSENT

All around the world there are laws about what age you are allowed to have sex. In some countries it is illegal to have homosexual sex.

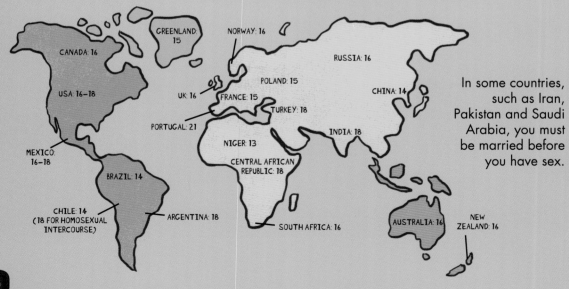

GREENLAND: 15

NORWAY: 16

CANADA: 16

RUSSIA: 16

USA: 16–18

POLAND: 15

CHINA: 14

UK: 16
FRANCE: 15

TURKEY: 18

PORTUGAL: 21

INDIA: 18

MEXICO: 16–18

NIGER: 13

CENTRAL AFRICAN REPUBLIC: 18

BRAZIL: 14

CHILE: 14 (18 FOR HOMOSEXUAL INTERCOURSE)

ARGENTINA: 18

SOUTH AFRICA: 16

AUSTRALIA: 16

NEW ZEALAND: 16

In some countries, such as Iran, Pakistan and Saudi Arabia, you must be married before you have sex.

A WHIRLWIND

Whatever your sexuality, the same whoosh of feelings is experienced and the rules about consent always apply. As does staying **safe** and being **protected**. Condoms* are the safest form of protection as they also protect against sexually transmitted diseases, such as chlamydia, as well as preventing pregnancy.

*Condoms are **98 per cent** effective for preventing pregnancy (if used properly). Other types of protection include: birth control pill, implant or injection, coil and diaphragm.

1. KISSING
2. TOUCHING
7. PUTTING ON A CONDOM
6. GIVING CONSENT
8. INTERCOURSE
3. HEAVY PETTING
5. LISTENING TO WHAT YOUR PARTNER WANTS
4. SAYING NO/ SAYING YES

THE RHYTHM OF SEXUAL INTERCOURSE

Sexual intercourse happens when a sexual organ penetrates or is penetrated by another organ.

Partners often move in rhythm together, building pleasure.

At the peak of sexual pleasure, one, neither or both partners may have an orgasm.

Orgasm may happen by stimulating the penis or clitoris.

When sex feels good, a release of hormones can make you feel happy, relaxed and in love.

If sex doesn't feel good then talk about it and get all your feelings out.

ARE YOU READY?

Use this Venn diagram to work out whether you are ready to have sex.

HAVE **FUN** TOGETHER

Enjoy your relationship, you're not ready for sex yet.

TRUST EACH OTHER

Wait until you fully trust each other.

HAVE SEX IF YOU FEEL READY

Have sex for the right reasons; are you really ready?

REACHED THE **AGE OF CONSENT**

MAKING BABIES!

1 x EGG + 1 x SPERM = 1 x BABY
(OR TWINS SOMETIMES!)

Sexual intercourse is just one part of making babies. Ejaculation releases semen containing sperm inside the vagina. Millions of sperm begin a journey through the female sexual organs on a mission to find an egg to fertilise.

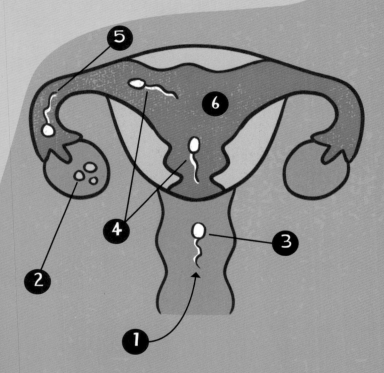

RACE FOR LIFE

1. Between **20–300 million sperm** enter the vagina. Sperm can survive here for up to **5 days**.

2. Usually **1 egg** is released from the ovaries per menstrual cycle. It journeys down a fallopian tube, but will live for only **24 hours**.

3. Sperm are built for speed. A long tail propels them at **16 kph**. Each sperm is on a mission of a lifetime to fertilise the egg.

4. Sperm race through the vagina, then into the cervix and uterus. Next, they swim into either fallopian tube.

5. Some sperm are fitter than others. Only **a few thousand** will reach the egg.

6. Usually **1 sperm** penetrates the wall of the egg. The now fertilised egg then implants itself in the uterus.

SPERM WARS!

There is a theory that on the journey up the fallopian tubes the sperm are not just racing to get to the egg, they are fighting, too! Killer Sperm and Blocker Sperm are waging war against Fertiliser Sperm.

NATURAL SELECTION

Scientists believe that the tough journey that sperm make is part of nature's selection process. If the strongest sperm becomes the one that fertilises the egg, the changes of creating a healthy baby are much higher.

KNOW YOUR EGGS

A **20-week-old female foetus** has around **7 million eggs!**

At birth, females have around **2 million eggs** in their ovaries.

Around **11,000 eggs** die every month before puberty.

When a girl starts her periods, she has around **300,000 to 500,000 eggs** left.

It takes **1 egg** to make a baby or identical twins.

It takes **2 eggs** to make non-identical twins.

20 WAYS TO SURVIVE PUBERTY

Check out these top tips to help you on your rollercoaster ride from child to adult.

1. **Growing up** and going through **puberty** *is* **exciting**. All those changes are amazing – even the hairy bits!

2. Sometimes the journey from childhood to adulthood will get a little bumpy, but never forget that **you are awesome**.

3. There are people who will help you through the tough times. **Family, friends** and **teachers** at school are there for you.

4. If things get really serious or **scary**, there are **self-help groups** or **specialist organisations** that can help, too (see page 47).

5. **Laugh** your socks off! Laughing releases powerful chemicals called endorphins, which make you feel **AMAZING**!

6. **Sing** in the shower, warble as you walk and rap in your room. Singing releases more of those feel-good chemicals called **endorphins**.

7. **Sleep deep.** You need **8–10 hours** of sleep to be in tip-top condition.

8. In the hour before bed, **90 per cent** of people use digital devices. It affects how long it takes to drop off and the quality of your snooze!

9. Feel fruity! Eat at least **5 portions of fruit and veg** every day.

10. Get water wise! **9–12-year-olds** need **1.5 litres** a day (**7 glasses**) and teenagers need **2 litres (8–10 glasses)**.

11. **Help others**. It's a proven scientific fact that **giving feels good**!

12. **Relax! Yoga** not only keeps your body stretched and supple, but it calms the mind and stabilises hormones.

13. Aim for at least **60 minutes** of activity of a **moderate intensity** every day, such as walking to school or riding a scooter.

14. **Vigorous activities** are important for developing **bone health** and **muscle strength**. Running, swimming or football **3 times a week** are great choices.

15. Cut down on **sugar**. It causes tooth decay and can lead to obesity and health problems, such as diabetes.

16. **Online safety** is vital. Make sure you know the **5 P's**: **P**asswords, **P**rivacy settings, **P**ersonal information, **P**rofiles, **P**adlocks.

17. See off the **cyberbullies. 1 in 3 young people** are bullied online and only **1 in 10** tell a trusted adult. Make sure you speak out!

18. Be aware that **pornography** is not like real life. Talk to an adult if you feel scared or confused.

19. **Consent matters!** The **first rule of safe sex** is don't have it until you reach the **age of consent**. And remember that before you have sex with anyone you must have **their consent**!

20. **Safe sex** means using **contraceptives. Condoms** protect against **pregnancy** and **sexually transmitted diseases (S.T.D.)**.

GLOSSARY

acne
large numbers of pimples caused by inflamed or infected sebaceous glands

areola
the area of raised skin around the nipple

bacteria
a microscopic single-celled organism. Many bacteria cause diseases.

chromosome
part of the nucleus of a human cell. It includes DNA and other information, which makes the cell grow and reproduce in a certain way.

climax
an orgasm

clitoris
a part of the female sex organs above the opening of the urethra. It's about the size of a pea and can feel pleasurable when it is touched.

contraceptive
a way of stopping babies being made. Another term for this is birth control and it includes barrier methods, such as using condoms or diaphragms or taking drugs like 'the pill'.

douche
a device for washing out the vagina

ejaculation
when a male has an orgasm and semen (sperm and seminal fluid) is released from the penis

erection
what happens when blood flow increases to the penis causing it to become larger and harder

exfoliate
to remove dead skin cells from the surface of the skin by gently rubbing it with a facial scrub

fertilise
to cause an egg to develop into a new individual living thing

foreskin
the fold of skin that covers the top end of the penis

genitals
the sex organs

glands
organs that release chemicals into the body

hormones
chemicals made in our bodies that send messages to the organs about how to behave

immune system
the cells in the human body that work together to protect us from disease or substances that cause disease

labia
the folds of skin around the entrance to the vagina

larynx
an organ in the throat that holds the vocal chords; the voice box

menstrual cup
a flexible rubber or silicone cup that is inserted into the vagina and catches the blood during a period

oestrogen
a sex hormone that causes the female characteristics of the body to develop

orgasm
the pleasurable feeling from touching and stimulating the sexual organs often peaks in intense bursts of pleasure felt mostly in the genitals. This is the point when males ejaculate sperm and everyone releases the 'hormones of happiness' called endorphins.

ovaries
female reproductive organs where eggs are stored

pornography
videos or photographs that display sexual organs or people having sex

protein
an essential part of our diet, which is found in foods such as meat, eggs and beans

pubic hair
hair that grows around the genitals of adults and most people going through puberty

scrotum
a pouch of skin that contains the testicles

testicles
male reproductive organs where sperm is produced and stored

testosterone
a sex hormone that causes the male characteristics of the body to develop

uterus
an organ in the female body where a baby grows before it is born; the womb

vitamins
chemicals that are essential for our bodies to grow and stay healthy

BOOKS TO READ

The A-Z of Growing Up, Puberty and Sex by Lesley De Meza and Stephen De Silva (Franklin Watts, 2018)

Dr Christian's Guide to Growing **by Dr Christian Jessen** (Scholastic, 2013)

Girls Only! by Victoria Parker (Hodder Children's Books, 2014)

The Boy Files: Puberty, Growing Up and All that Stuff by Alex Hooper-Hodson (Wayland, 2017)

The Girl Files: Puberty: All about puberty and growing up by Jacqui Bailey (Wayland, 2017)

The Boys' Guide to Growing Up **by Phil Wilkinson** (Wayland, 2017)

The Girls' Guide to Growing Up **by Anita Naik** (Wayland, 2017)

ORGANISATIONS TO HELP

NHS

There's lots of information about how to stay healthy and what is happening during the different stages of puberty on this website.

www.nhs.uk/live-well/sexual-health/stages-of-puberty-what-happens-to-boys-and-girls/

Brook

This website is all about sexual health and wellbeing for the under 25s or young people. Hot topics include contraception, pregnancy, relationships, gender, abuse and violence.

www.brook.org.uk/

Family Lives

Call the Family Lives helpline if you need support or advice about anything to do with puberty. This organisation really understands puberty and is here to help, offer tips and support anybody who is finding this a challenging time.

HELPLINE: 0808 800 2222

Runawayhelp

If puberty is seriously getting you down to the point that you feel like running away then this organisation offers free, confidential advice. Check out the website for videos and information about body changes, relationship advice etc.

www.runawayhelpline.org.uk

Call or text: 116 000

Email: 116000@runawayhelpline.org.uk

Place2Be

A charity that works with schools to provide support for improving the mental health and emotional wellbeing of children who are coping with difficult situations including bullying, family breakdown and trauma.

www.place2be.org.uk

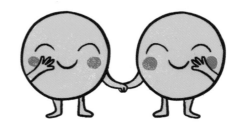

INDEX